THE MIDDLE AGES

NEW CONQUESTS AND DYNASTIES

Thanks to the creative team:
Senior Editor: Alice Peebles
Consultant: John Haywood
Fact Checking: Tom Jackson
Designer: Lauren Woods and collaborate agency

Original edition copyright 2018 by Hungry Tomato Ltd.
Copyright © 2018 by Lerner Publishing Group, Inc.

Hungry Tomato® is a trademark of Lerner Publishing Group

Hungry Tomato®
A division of Lerner Publishing Group, Inc.
241 First Avenue North
Minneapolis, MN 55401 USA

For reading levels and more information, look up
this title at www.lernerbooks.com.

Main body text set in Avenir Next Medium 10/12
Typeface provided by Linotype AG.

Library of Congress Cataloging-in-Publication Data

Names: Farndon, John, author. | Cornia, Christian, 1975- illustrator.
Title: The Middle Ages : new conquests and dynasties / written by John
          Farndon ; illustrated by Christian Cornia.
Description: Minneapolis : Hungry Tomato, [2018] | Series: Human history
          timeline | Includes index. | Audience: Grades 4-6.
Identifiers: LCCN 2017036911 (print) | LCCN 2017037166 (ebook)
          | ISBN 9781512498745 (eb pdf) | ISBN 9781512459722 (lb :
          alk. paper)
Subjects: LCSH: Middle Ages—Juvenile literature. | Middle Ages—
          Biography– Juvenile literature.
Classification: LCC D117 (ebook) | LCC D117 .F37 2018 (print) |
          DDC 909.07—dc23

LC record available at https://lccn.loc.gov/2017036911

Manufactured in the United States of America
1-43031-27700-10/5/2017

THE MIDDLE AGES

NEW CONQUESTS AND DYNASTIES

by John Farndon
Illustrated by Christian Cornia

HUNGRY TOMATO®

Minneapolis

CONTENTS

In the book, some dates have c. before them. This is short for "circa," or "about," showing that an exact date is not known. All dates up to 1000 are given as BCE or CE.

The Middle Ages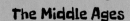

The Middle Ages are the time in the middle—between the collapse of the Roman world and the Renaissance 1,000 years later, when Greek and Roman ideas were rediscovered. And it's only called the Middle Ages in Europe. Everywhere else they have ages all their own.

Americas

Much of the Americas carried on quietly. But if you were in Central America, you may have fallen under the power of the empire of mighty Maya who built pyramids in the forest. And in the 1400s, you may have suffered at the hands of the savage Aztec Empire or the intimidating Incas.

NEW CONQUESTS AND DYNASTIES

When the Roman Empire fell in 476 CE, Europe became, well, a bit of a mess. People were far too disorganized to keep records in this time. That's why it's sometimes called the Dark Ages. It was a time for warriors on horseback with swords and armor rather than pen-pushing clerks. It was also a time when Christians built the first churches and abbeys and Muslims built mosques.

Asia

Japan had warlords and knights called shoguns and samurai, while Chinese empires were the most advanced in the world. But in 1206, ruthless horse warriors from Mongolia led by Chinggis (Genghis) Khan swept in and took over. The Mongols headed west too, destroying Muslim cities like Baghdad.

Europe

Vikings from Scandinavia brought terror everywhere they went. Roaming warlords claimed land and built castles to guard it. In the feudal system, the lords made poor serfs farm the land and, in return, kept knights to protect the serfs. At times, the knights went on Crusades to the Holy Land.

Eurasia

Eurasia was supercharged by the coming of Islam, the religion begun by the prophet Muhammad in Arabia in the 7th century. The Muslims soon created an empire of believers from Spain to India. They built fabulous mosques and cities, and their scholars made many advances in science.

Africa

In Africa, the spread of Islam transformed many places. In West Africa, magnificent empires, such as those of Mali and Songhai, were built on mining gold and salt, and African cities like Timbuktu rivalled many in Europe. In East Africa, Arabs arrived in sailing boats to trade, and sultans ruled from cities such as Zanzibar.

Map Key

★ On the maps, major battle are shown by this symbol.

King Arthur

Mythically c. 450–550 CE Britain

Legends tell of King Arthur, who led Britons to a great victory over invading Saxons and how he gathered knights at a round table. He may have been a Roman leader. But there is no proof he existed.

Iona, where St. Columba lived

Canterbury, where Archbishop Augustine lived

Map Key
- Britons
- Thuringians
- Franks
- Visigoths
- Ostrogoths
- Byzantine Empire

Toledo

Rome

Going Goth

c. 418–720 CE Spain

The Goths were tribes that probably came from Scandinavia. Visigoths made a kingdom in the West, in Spain and France, and Ostrogoths settled in the East. The Romans gave Goths a really bad press—maybe because in 410 CE, they wrecked Rome!

Great Gregory

590–604 CE Rome

When Pope Gregory I saw Angle (English) slave boys in a market in Rome, he said, "They are not Angles, but Angels." He freed them and sent St. Augustine to England to convert people to Christianity.

481 CE	**490 CE**	**493 CE**	**527 CE**	**541–542 CE**	**563 CE**
Clovis I becomes Frankish king	King Arthur's Battle of Mt. Badon	Theodoric becomes King of Italy	Justinian I becomes Byzantine emperor	Plague of Justinian	St. Columba founds Iona monastery

Augustine twice
Algeria and England

About this time there were *two* Augustines: 4th-century Aug. was a great thinker from Hippo in Algeria; 6th-century Aug. brought Christianity to England and became the first Archbishop of Canterbury.

Hippo, where St. Augustine lived

Aksum

Just Aksum
c. 100–940 CE Ethiopia

The city and kingdom of Aksum was a powerful trader on the route between Rome and India. The people liked to build granite pillars, including one 79 ft. (24 m) high, in what is now the city of Axum.

Women of Constantinople, stricken with the plague, seeking help from the bishop

KINGS AND CHRISTIANS
476–600 CE

Without Rome as top dog, warlords carved out kingdoms in Europe: Clovis became king in France, Theodoric in Germany, and the legendary Arthur in Britain. Many became Christian. Clovis was converted to Christianity by his queen, Clothilde. There were people recognized as saints too, like Irish saints Columba, Patrick, and Brigid.

Deadly plague
541–542 CE Constantinople

The Justinian Plague, named after Emperor Justinian, ravaged Constantinople and spread west and east. It killed 25 million people—a seventh of all the people in the world!

565 CE	**570 CE**	**577 CE**	**589 CE**	**590 CE**	**593 CE**
Death of Byzantine general Belisarius	Birth of Prophet Muhammad	Matches invented in China	Sui dynasty reunites China	Gregory the Great becomes pope	Suiko is Japan's first empress

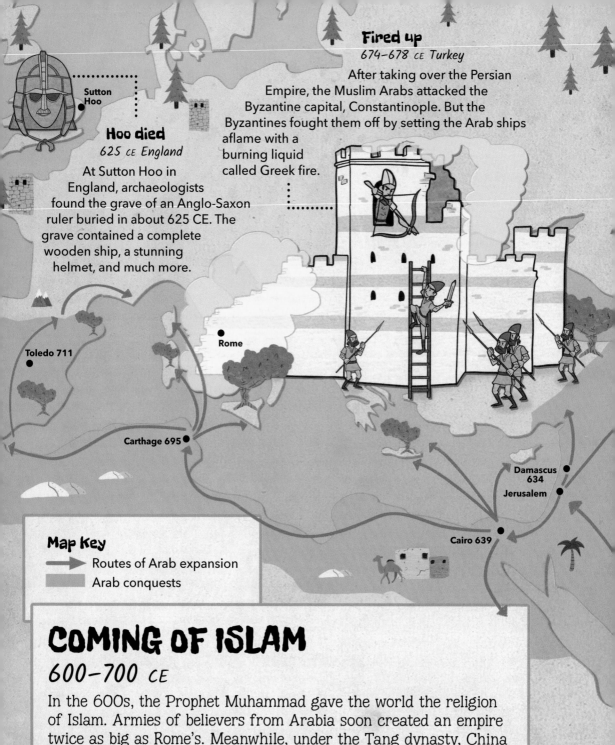

Fired up
674–678 CE Turkey

After taking over the Persian Empire, the Muslim Arabs attacked the Byzantine capital, Constantinople. But the Byzantines fought them off by setting the Arab ships aflame with a burning liquid called Greek fire.

Sutton Hoo

Hoo died
625 CE England

At Sutton Hoo in England, archaeologists found the grave of an Anglo-Saxon ruler buried in about 625 CE. The grave contained a complete wooden ship, a stunning helmet, and much more.

Toledo 711

Rome

Carthage 695

Damascus 634

Jerusalem

Cairo 639

Map Key
→ Routes of Arab expansion
⬛ Arab conquests

COMING OF ISLAM
600–700 CE

In the 600s, the Prophet Muhammad gave the world the religion of Islam. Armies of believers from Arabia soon created an empire twice as big as Rome's. Meanwhile, under the Tang dynasty, China became the world's most advanced civilization.

610 CE
Heraclius becomes Byzantine emperor

615 CE
Persian Khosrow II captures Jerusalem

615 CE
Pacal rules the Maya city of Palenque

618 CE
Tang dynasty begins in China

622 CE
Year one of the Muslim calendar

625 CE
Sutton Hoo burial in England

Wu did it
660–705 CE China

Wu Zetian was the only woman to rule China as empress. She took control when her husband, Emperor Gaozong, died while their son was too young to rule. She was said to have been a strong but kind ruler.

Buddhism rules
593–622 CE Japan

Young Prince Shotoku is said to have governed Japan for his aunt, Empress Suiko. Shotoku introduced Buddhism and the teachings of the Chinese thinker Confucius to Japan.

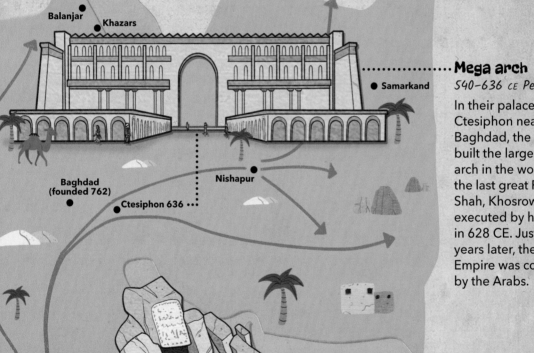

Balanjar

Khazars

Samarkand

Mega arch
540–636 CE Persia (Iraq)

In their palace at Ctesiphon near modern Baghdad, the Persians built the largest brick arch in the world. Here, the last great Persian Shah, Khosrow II, was executed by his son in 628 CE. Just eight years later, the Persian Empire was conquered by the Arabs.

Baghdad (founded 762)

Nishapur

Ctesiphon 636

God's messenger
610 CE Saudi Arabia

The Prophet Muhammad often went to think in a cave called Hira outside his home city of Mecca. Here, according to Islam, he was visited by the Archangel Gabriel who revealed the message of the Koran to him.

Medina

Mecca 622

| **627 CE** Emperor Heraclius defeats the Persians | **636 CE** Muslims conquer Persia | **674 CE** First Arab siege of Constantinople | **680 CE** Battle of Karbala divides Islam | **690 CE** Wu becomes empress of China | **691 CE** China becomes Buddhist |

Raiders from the sea

793 CE England

The Vikings in their swift longships could strike anywhere! In 793, they burnt down the Christian monastery at Lindisfarne in England. Vikings also ventured into Ukraine and Russia.

Big Charlie's church!

796 CE Germany

Charlemagne (Charles the Great) was a Christian and conquered Germany and Italy. So the Pope crowned him Holy Roman Emperor. Charlemagne ordered a great cathedral to be built at Aachen.

Tours

ANDALUS

Andalus

c. 711 CE–1492

Muslims from North Africa took over what is now Spain and Portugal. They called the land Al-Andalus and built great cities, such as Cordoba. But at Tours, the Franks stopped their push into France. After that they kept to Spain.

Ghana gold

c.400 CE–1200 Ghana

Thanks to camels, Ghana grew rich trading gold across the Sahara with Muslim merchants. The capital of the Ghana Empire was at Koumbi Saleh on the edge of the desert.

711 CE	**711 CE**	**712 CE**	**732 CE**	**742 CE**	**750 CE**
Muslims conquer Spain	Maya city of Palenque conquered	Emperor Xuanzong rules in China	Battle of Tours won by Charles Martel	China is home to over 1 million	Muslim Abbasid dynasty replaces the Umayyads

ARABS AND VIKINGS
700–800 CE

The Arabs spread Muslim rule from Spain to China. But in France they lost a key battle against the Franks, who soon created a new Roman empire in Europe under their king, Charlemagne. Meanwhile, terrifying Viking seafarers raided ever farther from their Scandinavian homeland.

Tang bang! *c. 800 CE China*

In the time of the Tang emperors, the Chinese learned to make explosions with gunpowder. At first, they just made fireworks. Then they found out how to fire rockets at enemies. Their secret reached Europe four centuries later.

Arabian nights

c. 786–809 CE Baghdad

Under Caliph Harun al-Rashid, brilliant scholars translated great works by Greek thinkers and made new discoveries. The Caliph was entertained by the tales of *One Thousand and One Nights*.

Borobudur

760–825 CE Indonesia

The world's largest Buddhist temple was begun in the 8th century. After 500 years, it was abandoned and only rediscovered in the jungle in 1814.

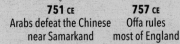

751 CE	**757 CE**	**760 CE**	**762 CE**	**772 CE**	**793 CE**
Arabs defeat the Chinese near Samarkand	Offa rules most of England	Borobudur temple, Indonesia, started	Baghdad founded	Charlemagne's Frankish Empire begins	Viking raid on Lindisfarne Abbey

KINGDOMS OF THE NORTH

800–900 CE

New nations started to emerge in Europe. Scotland had its first king, Kenneth McAlpin. King Alfred defied the Vikings to help make England. The Frankish empire split into what in time would be France and Germany. Viking Rurik created the first Russia, Kievan Rus, and Boris I founded Bulgaria.

England and Iceland
871–899 CE

Anglo-Saxon king Alfred the Great drove out the Vikings, and England became united. Later, some intrepid Vikings reached Iceland, settled there, and created the oldest parliament, the Althing, in 930 CE.

ICELAND

Winchester

Cordoba

Fatima's books
859 CE Morocco

Fatima al-Fihri, a merchant's daughter in the city of Fez, set up what is now the world's oldest library, Al Quaraouiyine. She started a kind of university there, the world's first.

Maya mystery
c. 850 CE

After thousands of years, the main centers of Maya civilization in Mexico collapsed. People vanished for no known reason, leaving their great temples to be overgrown by the jungle.

794 CE	**809 CE**	**810 CE**	**814 CE**	**841 CE**	**846 CE**
Heian-kyō (Kyoto) is capital of Japan	Byzantines make war on Bulgarians	Kenneth McAlpin, the first Scots king	Charlemagne dies	Dublin founded by the Vikings	Arab raid on Rome

Charles the Fat *884–887 CE Germany*

Charles the Fat was said to be very lazy. Yet for a short while his Carolingian Empire in western Europe was the biggest since the Romans.

Fujiwaras
794 CE–1145 Japan

For 350 years, Japan was ruled not by emperors but by the Fujiwara family. The Fujiwaras made sure each emperor married one of their daughters.

Bulgarian Boris
852–889 CE Bulgaria

Eastern Europe was torn between two centers of Christianity: Rome in the West and Constantinople. Bulgaria's King Boris I made friends with Constantinople. He turned Bulgaria Christian and ruled a Bulgarian empire.

Kiev

Rome

Pliska

Constantinople

Damascus

IRAN

Chola roller
850–870 CE India

The Chola people of southern India are the ancestors of today's Tamil. They first appeared around 300 BCE. But in 850 CE, their king, Vijayayala, created a great empire that lasted four centuries.

Arab stars
c. 828 CE

Muslims needed to know the time to pray and which way to face, so they used the stars for guidance. In 828 CE, they built an astronomical observatory at Shammasiyah in Baghdad. Later, they built a famous one at Maragheh in Iran (*shown*).

862 CE
Rurik establishes Kievan Rus

863 CE
Chinese author describes eastern Africa

c. 870 CE
Vikings settle in Iceland

872 CE
Harald Fairhair unites Norway

878 CE
Alfred defeats the Danes at Ethandun

885 CE
In Bulgaria, St Cyril creates alphabet

Viking Vinland
985 CE Newfoundland

Viking sagas tell how Viking seafarers saw America in 985 CE. A band led by Leif Erikson later settled there, calling it Vinland.

Otto power
955 CE

The Magyars' takeover of central Europe was stopped at the Battle of Lechfeld by German king Otto the Great. Otto became the Holy Roman Emperor.

Vinland

Rolf the Ganger
911 CE France

Even the tough Franks couldn't stop the Vikings, or Northmen, claiming Normandy in northern France. The Normans' first ruler was called Rolf the Ganger (walker)—he was so big no horse would carry him!

NORMANDY   **Lechfeld**

Rome

Cordoba

VIKINGS EVERYWHERE
900 CE-1000

In the 10th century, the Vikings were a pretty dynamic bunch. They sailed to North America and settled there. They made northern France their own. They set themselves up in Russia and made that their own too. They even got to be the Byzantine emperor's personal guards!

Map Key
➤ Migrations and raids
▢ Area of Viking activity

895 CE	c. 900 CE	911 CE	927 CE	936 CE	c. 950 CE
Magyars settle in Pannonia (Hungary)	Hidesato, legendary Japanese warrior	Viking Normandy created	England unified	Gorm the Old, first king of Denmark	Lions die out in Europe

Making money 960 CE China

The Chinese were short of copper for coins, and people were fed up with carrying heavy coins. So the Song government issued paper notes called *jiaozi*, the first bank notes. A jiaozi was a promise to pay.

Chang'an

Novgorod

RUSSIA

The making of Russia 988 CE

Russia was united by heroic Vladimir, prince of Novgorod. As Vladimir the Great, he established the nation.

Kiev

Spinning around c. 900 CE China/India

In ancient times, people made yarn (thread for weaving cloth) by spinning fibers together by hand on a stick, or distaff. Then the spinning wheel was invented. It was turned by pedal, making the process faster, and leaving hands free.

Constantinople

The V men 988 CE Turkey

From the age of 10, Vikings learned to fight with bows, spears, and swords. Byzantine emperors hired them as bodyguards, known as the Varangian Guard. They had long hair and wore ruby earrings and chain mail coats with dragon images.

Baghdad

c. 951 CE
Muslim scholar
al-Farabi dies

955 CE
German victory at
Lechfeld

962 CE
Otto the Great Holy
Roman Emperor

977 CE
Persian poem
Shahnameh begun

987 CE
Hugh Capet first
Capetian king of France

988 CE
Vladimir I of Rus
becomes Christian

Norman invasion *1066 England*

A fortnight after beating off a Viking attack, England's King Harold was defeated by Normans from France, led by William the Conqueror. Harold was killed, and William became king of England. The invading Normans built castles all over England and Wales to keep the local Anglo-Saxons in check.

Stamford Bridge

Hastings

Cross knights
1099

The pope's call for a crusade led to huge armies of knights and peasants leaving the land in western Europe. They trekked for months until they reached Constantinople. They then went on to Jerusalem, captured the city, and slaughtered the city's Muslims and Jews.

Bologna

Rome

Constantinople

Jerusalem

Scholars rule
1088 Italy

In ancient times, people had learned from private tutors. But in 1088, Europe saw its first university, at Bologna in Italy where scholars could come together to study with the best. Eight years later, Oxford University was founded.

Big split
1054

After centuries of tension, the Christians in Rome and the Christians in Constantinople finally decided to divorce in 1054. The split was called the Great Schism, and Christianity became divided between Catholics in the West and Orthodox Christians in the East.

c.1001	**1011**	**1016**	**1025**	**1040**	**1041**
The Japanese *Tale of Genji*	High King Brian Boru unites Ireland	Cnut the Great is king of England	Avicenna's *The Canon of Medicine*	Macbeth becomes king of Scotland	Movable type invented

CONQUEST AND COLLAPSE
1000–1100

In 1066, the Normans of France conquered England. But this was just a sideshow to the coming showdown between Christians and Muslims. It all kicked off when the Byzantines asked for help against the Turks. In reply, Pope Urban II called for a crusade, a warlike pilgrimage to the Holy Land.

Snaky!
1070 Ohio, North America

The Great Serpent Mound was built by people called the Fort Ancient Culture. Some suggest it was for astronomy as it was made when a supernova (exploding star) and a comet were seen.

Storybook romance
1021 Japan

Muraskai Shikibu was a lady-in-waiting at the Japanese court. She wrote the first-ever novel, *The Tale of Genji*. It was the clever story of the loves of Prince Genji.

Map Key

→ First Crusade

1066	1088	1093	1094	1095	1099
Norman Conquest of England	University of Bologna founded	Kypchaks defeat Kievan Rus	Spanish hero El Cid conquers Valencia	Pope Urban calls for a crusade	Siege of Jerusalem by crusaders

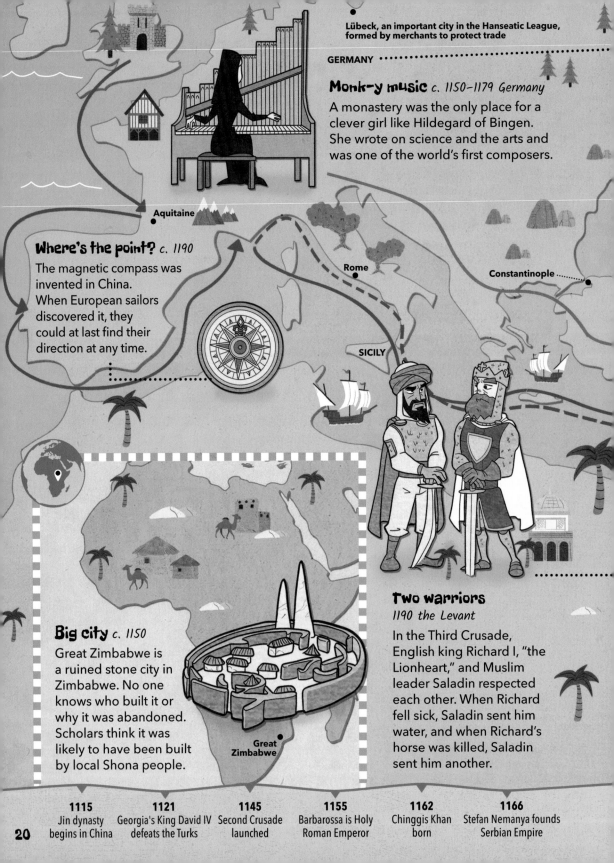

Lübeck, an important city in the Hanseatic League, formed by merchants to protect trade

GERMANY

Monk-y music *c. 1150–1179 Germany*

A monastery was the only place for a clever girl like Hildegard of Bingen. She wrote on science and the arts and was one of the world's first composers.

Aquitaine

Rome

Constantinople

Where's the point? *c. 1190*

The magnetic compass was invented in China. When European sailors discovered it, they could at last find their direction at any time.

SICILY

Two warriors
1190 the Levant

In the Third Crusade, English king Richard I, "the Lionheart," and Muslim leader Saladin respected each other. When Richard fell sick, Saladin sent him water, and when Richard's horse was killed, Saladin sent him another.

Big city *c. 1150*

Great Zimbabwe is a ruined stone city in Zimbabwe. No one knows who built it or why it was abandoned. Scholars think it was likely to have been built by local Shona people.

Great Zimbabwe

1115	1121	1145	1155	1162	1166
Jin dynasty begins in China	Georgia's King David IV defeats the Turks	Second Crusade launched	Barbarossa is Holy Roman Emperor	Chinggis Khan born	Stefan Nemanya founds Serbian Empire

Heavy metal
1155–1190 Germany

Frederick Barbarossa (Redbeard) was a tough German king who became Holy Roman Emperor. He refused to be bossed by the pope and set up an antipope in protest. But in 1190 he drowned crossing a river in Turkey.

In Europe this was a time of soaring cathedrals, mighty castles, and serene monasteries. It was also a time when merchants made markets exciting places and knights went off to fight crusades. In the Islamic world, learning reached new peaks in sophisticated cities.

Crusader Routes
→ Richard the Lionheart
→ Frederick Barbarossa

CYPRUS
Hattin

Cairo
Jerusalem

Fighters and bankers
1119

Many pilgrims traveled to the temple at Jerusalem, and the Knights Templar were set up to protect them. These knights were crack fighters and became Europe's first bankers by looking after pilgrims' money.

Shogun power
1192

In Japan, emperors were often weak, and in 1192 a war leader, or shogun, called Minamoto Yoritomo took over. For the next 700 years, it was always a shogun who really ran Japan, even though there was an emperor.

1168	1170	1187	1189	1192	1192
Antipope Callixtus III challenges the pope	Archbishop Thomas Becket murdered	Saladin wins Jerusalem	Third Crusade launched	Minamoto the first shogun in Japan	Richard I defeats Saladin at Jaffa

Battle on the ice 1242 Estonia
The Teutonic (German) knights were defeated on a frozen lake by Russians under Alexander Nevsky.

Great charter 1215 England
English barons were fed up with King John's bossy ways. So they made him sign the Magna Carta (Great Charter), with rules for his behavior.

London

Kiev

MONGOL EMPIRE

FRANCE

Vienna

Constantinople

Toledo

Cordoba

Moorish al-Andalus

Baghdad

PERSIA

Fighting for Spain 1212
At Las Navas de Tolosa, Christians won a key battle in the Reconquista: the Christian fight to take Spain back from Moors (Muslims). A shepherd led them secretly through a gorge to catch the Moors by surprise.

Mali might c. 1235–1610
In the Middle Ages, everyone wanted gold, and Mali in western Africa had more than anyone. With the money from gold, Mali created a vast empire, and their mightiest ruler, Mansa Muta (1312–1337), was by far the richest man in the world.

MALI

1206	1215	1233	1235	1240	1241
Chinggis Khan is Mongol leader	English king John signs Magna Carta	Mongols conquer Kaifeng in China	Mali Empire is formed	Mongols conquer Russia	Mongols conquer Hungarians and Poles

MONGOL HORDES
1200–1300

This century is the amazing story of Temujin, a poor nomad boy from remote central Asia. Temüjin made himself leader of the Mongols as Chinggis Khan. As Chinggis, he led the ferocious Mongol hordes east into China and west into the Islamic Empire to create the greatest land empire ever.

Kublai Khan
1260–1294

Under Chinggis's grandson, Kublai Khan, the Mongols took over China. In fact, Kublai Khan became Chinese emperor, starting an entirely new dynasty named the Yuan.

Mongol slaughter 1200s

The Mongols built a vast empire by terrifying people. They swept down on cities on their horses and slaughtered everyone, killing tens of millions of people and wrecking cities like Baghdad.

Karakorum

Kaifeng

Samarkand

CHINA

Traveler's tales 1300 Italy

Venetian traveler Marco Polo visited China in the late 1200s, and wrote about his adventures at Kublai Khan's court in *The Travels of Marco Polo*. It inspired Columbus to try to get to China 200 years later by sailing west.

1242	**1258**	**1279**	**1295**	**1297**	**1299**
Russians conquer Teutonic knights	Mongols destroy Baghdad	Kublai Khan conquers all China	Marco Polo returns from China	William Wallace, Guardian of Scotland	Ottoman Empire begins

Revolting peasants

1381 England

Peasants led by Wat Tyler marched to London to protest about their tough lives. The Lord Mayor killed Wat, but King Richard II promised to meet their demands. They went home happy, but the king's men then hanged them all.

Hundred Years' War

1337–1453 France

England and France warred for over 100 years because the English Plantagenet kings thought they should rule France too. Archers helped the English win famous victories at Crécy (1346) and Agincourt (1415), but the French won in the end.

London

Tenochtitlán

Lake city *1325*

After upsetting a local king, the Mexica people built their city on artificial islands out in the middle of Lake Texcoco. Called Tenochtitlán, it became the greatest city in America at the time and the heart of the mighty Aztec Empire.

PLAGUE AND REBELLION
1300–1400

In the 14th century, the world was struck by a terrible disease called the bubonic plague, or the Black Death. It was the worst illness ever, killing up to 200 million people from China to Europe.

1299	1314	1325	1337	1342	1346
Osman I is first Ottoman emperor	Scots beat the English at Bannockburn	Aztecs found the city of Tenochtitlán	Hundred Years' War begins	Louis the Great is king of Hungary	English defeat the French at Crécy

Black Death
1347–1353
Europe and Asia

The Black Death was a deadly disease that reached Europe. It began when Mongol armies attacking Kaffa in Crimea catapulted infected corpses into the city. This plague killed millions of people.

Paris

FRANCE

Venice

Crimea

Constantinople

Bukhara

Samarkand

Eastern triumph
1451–1481 Turkey

Mehmet the Conqueror was the brilliant sultan (leader) of the Turkish Ottoman people. In 1453, he captured Constantinople and ended the Byzantine Empire. He made the city, now called Istanbul, his capital and then conquered large areas to create the powerful Ottoman Empire.

Lame Timur
1370–1405
central Asia

The dream of Timurlane (Timur the lame) was to re-create Chinggis Khan's empire. He was a talented leader and created a vast empire in central Asia. But his wars cost 17 million lives.

Map Key
→ Spread of the plague

1347	1363	1370	1378	1380	1381
Black Death strikes	Battle of Lake Poyang, China	Timur is emperor in Central Asia	Schism (split) of the Catholic Church	Charles the Mad is king of France	Peasants' Revolt in England

Wars of the Roses
1455–1487 England

The families of York and Lancaster fought the Wars of the Roses over who should rule England. The Lancaster symbol was a white rose, the York, a red rose.

Is this China?
1492 Bahamas

Christopher Columbus hoped to reach the Indies by crossing the unknown Atlantic. When all seemed lost, he made land at the Bahamas. He thought it was the Indies, but he'd only made it to the Americas!

Vienna

Castillon

Bahamas

High Inca
1438–1533 Peru

The Inca people of Peru created a huge empire stretching down western South America. They were amazing stoneworkers and created the extraordinary stone city of Macchu Picchu on a mountaintop.

Saintly Joan
1412–1431 France

Joan of Arc believed God had chosen her to fight the English. She led France to victory at Orléans but was captured by the English, tried, and burned at the stake, aged just 19.

Cannon power
1499 Greece

The Ottomans competed with Venetians to control the Mediterranean. In 1499 the two fought a battle in the Ionian Sea at Zonchio—the first sea battle in which cannons were fired.

1405	1410	1415	1415	1429	1453
Voyages of Admiral Zheng He	Teutonic knights beaten at Grunwald	English defeat the French at Agincourt	Czech rebel Jan Hus burned at stake	Joan of Arc lifts the siege of Orléans	Constantinople falls to the Ottomans

VOYAGERS AND EXPLORERS
1400-1500

In 1453 the Ottoman Turks captured Constantinople, blocking Europe's route to China and the Indies (Indonesia) with their spices and silks. Ships were sent out from Spain and Portugal to find a way around, starting an amazing age of discovery, with Christopher Columbus reaching the Americas in 1492.

Czech out
1419-1436 Czech Republic

Jan Hus was a Czech hero and priest who was burned at the stake when he protested about church corruption to the Holy Roman Emperor. The outraged Czech people then began the long Hussite Wars.

Constantinople

China ships
1405-1407 China

The Chinese didn't send out just a few small ships exploring, as Europeans did. In 1405 under Admiral Zheng He, they sent out hundreds of giant ships. They reached Africa, but the Chinese decided they had all they needed at home. The voyages stopped in 1533.

Explorers' routes
→ Christopher Columbus   → Zheng He
→ Ferdinand Magellan   → Vasco da Gama

1453	1455	1462	1469	1492	1497
Battle of Castillon ends Hundred Years' War	Wars of the Roses begin in England	Ottomans driven back by Vlad the Impaler	Ferdinand and Isabella unify Spain	Columbus reaches the Americas	Vasco da Gama sails to India

WHO'S WHO

Many different peoples lived in the Middle Ages. You must have heard about the Vikings and the Incas. But just who were they? And who were the others you've met in this book?

French or German: Franks
c. 300–800 CE

The Franks were Germanic peoples who took over most of western Europe after the Romans left. They split into two halves: the western Franks who became the French and the eastern Franks who became the Germans.

c. 300 CE

Gothic horror: Goths
394–775 CE

The Goths were Germanic people who migrated west from their homelands around the Baltic Sea to invade the Roman Empire. They include Visigoths (the western Goths) and Ostrogoths (the eastern Goths).

Thunderbolts from Asia: Mongols
1206–1368

The Mongols are nomadic people from central Asia. They are famous for the vast empire they created in the 13th century under the leadership of Khans, sweeping down in vast hordes on horseback to cause terrible slaughter.

People from the North: Normans
900 CE–1150

The Normans were Vikings (Norsemen) who settled in northern France. From there, they conquered England in 1066 and places in the Mediterranean, such as Sicily.

Eastern power: Ottomans
1299–1923

The Ottomans came from northwest Anatolia in modern Turkey. When the Islamic Empire collapsed, the Ottomans captured Constantinople and created their own huge empire.

Who's for more? Moors
711 CE–1492

Moors were the Muslim people of North Africa, Spain, and Portugal who were originally Berbers and Arabs. The word was used loosely by Europeans to describe any Muslim from these areas, but it covered a wide variety of people.

Sea wolves: Vikings
770 CE–1100

The Vikings, or Norsemen, were people from Scandinavia who raided and traded far across Europe. They were famous for their longships and seafaring skills and sailed all the way to North America to settle.

Interesting angles: Anglo-Saxons
410 CE–1066

The Anglo-Saxons were Germanic peoples who migrated to Britain in the 5th century. They quickly took over most of what is now England from the original Celtic inhabitants, or Britons. But they were faced by constant attack from the Vikings and were finally conquered by the Normans in 1066.

Russian forebears: Kievan Rus
882 CE–1240

Kievan Rus was the forerunner of Russia. It was a loose collection of Slavic people brought together by the Viking Rurik rulers and centered on Kiev. It collapsed in 1240 when it was overrun by the Mongols.

Hungry people: Magyars
800 CE–1000

The Magyars were Turkic people who came originally from the Urals in Russia. In the 9th and 10th centuries, they invaded the center of Europe and settled in what is now Hungary.

Cuzco we can: Incas
1438–1533

The Incas built a huge empire from their capital city Cuzco, high up in the Andean Mountains. They had no wheels or horses but built remarkable stone roads for walking.

Mex 'tecs: Aztecs
1427–1521

The Aztecs created a powerful empire from their lake city Tenochtitlán where Mexico City is now. They were ruthless soldiers who made mass human sacrifices of their enemies to keep their gods happy.

1533

WELL, I NEVER...

Some strange stories from the Middle Ages

HAVE I MADE MY POINT?

The name of the evil vampire Count Dracula was inspired by Vlad Dracula (1428–1477), a real-life Romanian prince. He led the resistance against the Ottoman invaders but became famous for his cruelty. He was called Vlad the Impaler because he would impale his victims on long wooden stakes.

GOOD KING

Wenceslas I, Duke of Bohemia (Czech Republic), was assassinated in 935 CE. But he became such a legend for his goodness that he was made a saint. One story tells how he offered to fight the enemy general Radislas single-handedly to stop soldiers getting hurt. But as Radislas came for him, angels intervened. Radislas fell on his knees before Wenceslas, asking for forgiveness.

ALL TIDE UP

The Viking Cnut the Great (995 CE-1035) was the only king to rule Norway, Denmark, and England. He was a wise king by all accounts. One famous legend tells how he tried to stop the tide coming in to show his courtiers that even his power had limits.

BLOWING UP AN ELEPHANT

A famous poem from the Middle Ages tells of Roland, a hero in the army of Charlemagne. In it, Roland's small troop is ambushed by Moors in the mountain pass of Roncesvalles in 778 CE. Not wanting to seem a coward, Roland refuses to blow his horn Olifant (elephant) to summon help. Then, with his last breath, he blows the horn, but it is too late.

BLUE TOOTH

Harald Blåtand was a 10th century Viking king who brought Christianity to the Danes and went a long way to creating the nation of Denmark. Apparently he was very good at bringing people together in a peaceful way. That's why the inventors of Bluetooth electronics named their system after him. Blåtand means "blue tooth"—and Harald may actually have had a blue tooth.

DON'T LISTEN TO ME: I'M CRAZY!

Brilliant Muslim scientist Alhazen (Ibn al-Haitham, 965-1040) was ordered to go to Egypt by the Caliph to stop the River Nile flooding. Alhazen came up with a scheme, but then, realizing it wouldn't work, pretended to be mad to escape the Caliph's anger. While hiding in his room faking craziness, he began to study light and wrote a groundbreaking book about what light is.

INDEX

The Author

John Farndon is Royal Literary Fellow at City&Guilds in London, UK, and the author of a huge number of books for adults and children on science, technology, and history, including international bestsellers. He has been shortlisted six times for the Royal Society's Young People's Book Prize, with titles such as *How the Earth Works* and *What Happens When?*

The Illustrator

Italian-born Christian Cornia decided at the age of four to be a comic-book artist and is essentially self-taught. He works digitally, but he always has a sketchbook in his bag. Cornia has illustrated Marvel Comics and is one of the artists for the Scooby-Doo character in Italy and the United States. He also teaches animation at the Scuola Internazionale di Comics in Italy.